W9-BYH-541

MORRIS AREA LIBRARY

High School Musicals ™

ACTING
From Audition to Performance

Bethany Bezdecheck

rosen publishing's
rosen central ®

New York

For my twin sister, Heather, a great actress and teacher

Published in 2010 by The Rosen Publishing Group, Inc.
29 East 21st Street, New York, NY 10010

Copyright © 2010 by The Rosen Publishing Group, Inc.

First Edition

All rights reserved. No part of this book may be reproduced in any form without permission in writing from the publisher, except by a reviewer.

Library of Congress Cataloging-in-Publication Data

Bezdecheck, Bethany.
Acting: from audition to performance / Bethany Bezdecheck. — 1st ed.
    p. cm. — (High school musicals)
Includes bibliographical references and index.
ISBN-13: 978-1-4358-5256-3 (library binding)
ISBN-13: 978-1-4358-5526-7 (pbk)
ISBN-13: 978-1-4358-5527-4 (6 pack)
1. Musicals—Instruction and study. 2. Acting. I. Title.
MT956.B49 2009
782.1'407—dc22

2008044019

Manufactured in Malaysia

3 9957 00151 5499

Contents

INTRODUCTION

Do you practice signing your autograph on a daily basis? Are you the type to make a big entrance? Have you already written your Academy Award acceptance speech? Do your friends and family refer to you as having "a dramatic personality"?

If any of these symptoms sound familiar, you may have been bitten by the acting bug! Unfortunately, there remains but one antidote to the acting bug's powerful bite: a career in show business. Luckily for you, high school students have easy access to "the business they call show." Today, almost every high school puts on an annual musical. If you've been thinking about taking the stage, all you have to do is seek out this year's audition. Before you can say, "Break a leg," you'll be on your way to theatrical success.

Did you know that many famous actors got their start in high school plays and musicals? Take Katie Holmes of the blockbuster film

In her high school's production of *Damn Yankees*, movie star Katie Holmes played Lola, the devil's seductress assistant. Not long afterward, she was starring in the hit television show *Dawson's Creek*.

Batman Begins, for example. Holmes actually declined auditioning in person for the TV show *Dawson's Creek* because she was too busy starring in her high school's production of the musical *Damn Yankees*. Ultimately impressed by Holmes's commitment to her high school's drama program, the producers decided to cast her anyway! Academy Award winner Morgan Freeman was also a high school thespian. The winner of a statewide drama competition at just twelve years of age, he was offered a drama scholarship by Jackson State University while still in high school.

Becoming a real show biz success like Holmes or Freeman takes more than just talent. Actors who are continually cast have had to learn and perfect various tricks of the trade. They understand the importance of audition etiquette, character development, and overall stage presence, which is the way in which an actor presents himself or herself onstage. This book aims to provide you with these tools and more. With its guidance, you will be one step ahead of the competition and one step closer to becoming an accomplished actor. Are you ready to take show business seriously? If so, keep perfecting that autograph, keep writing those acceptance speeches, and most important, keep reading!

Acing the Acting Audition

The first stage of every high school musical is the audition. At the audition, you and all others interested in participating in the musical will perform for the director. The purpose of the audition is for the director to get a sense of what type of performer you are and how to best cast you in the show. Whether you are determined to be assigned a lead role or would be happy with just a small role, the audition is the time for you to prove to the director that you have what it takes. But, in acting, there is no such thing as standing in the background. If you want to be onstage, you must be prepared to give it your all. A halfhearted performance will not get you cast.

Musicals require the entire cast to act, sing, and dance, so you can expect to do all three of these things at the audition. This knowledge may cause some actors to despair. Maybe you're thinking, "But I'm a terrible dancer!" or, "But people say I sound like a dying cat when I sing!" Don't worry! The director does not expect to see many "triple threats," or performers who are talented at acting, singing, and dancing, at the audition. Triple threats are extremely rare and are not always necessary for successful musical productions. Many musicals feature characters that are not required to sing or dance, at least not by themselves. However, even if you choose to audition for these types of roles only, you must still sing

With a little training, even an inexperienced dancer may be able to perform impressive moves by the time a show opens.

and dance for the director. It is important that you show him or her that you are at least willing to make an effort. Plus, you never know—the director may see you as having potential. He or she may feel that with a little training, you could be a real triple threat by the time the show opens!

Preparing for Your Audition

When you arrive at the audition, it is important for you to be dressed appropriately. Wear clothes that you are able to move freely in. Bring dance shoes, or lightweight shoes with rubber soles that will move easily across the floor. If you have long hair, make sure it is out of your face. You will want the director to be able to see your expression while you are acting. Leave flashy jewelry at home. It tends to catch the light onstage and therefore can be distracting. Although you should dress comfortably, you must not appear sloppy or disheveled. If you want to be taken seriously, it is important to look put together.

For the acting portion of the audition, you will most likely perform either a monologue (a speech given by one character) or a side (a section of a scene that includes two or more characters). If you are asked to perform a monologue, you may be required to have one prepared ahead of time. This type of preparation requires about two weeks' worth of research and practice, so plan accordingly.

There are books of monologues in print, some of which have been written or compiled specifically for young actors. Visit your local library and ask for help in finding one. However, before you do so, you should familiarize yourself with the show for which you will be auditioning. If it is a comedy, you will want to select a comedic monologue so that you can showcase your comedic abilities. If it is a drama, you should choose a monologue that is more serious so that you can exhibit a range of emotions. You should also give some thought as to which part you most want to play. If you would like to be cast as the handsome young prince, you will want to perform a monologue that allows you to display your goodness and charm. If you are hoping to play the part of the hideous ogre, you may want to look for a monologue meant for a less likable character. If you are not familiar with the show itself, you may be able to check out the script at the library as well.

Your monologue must be memorized by the time you audition. You will give a better performance if you do not have to look down at a script. Work on memorizing a couple of lines from your monologue each day. Practice reciting the monologue for friends or family, or in front of a mirror. Keep in mind the following as you rehearse:

Study yourself as you practice your monologue in front of a mirror. Do you appear stiff or at ease? Are you using too many hand gestures or too few? The more relaxed you are, the more natural your performance will appear.

Clarity and projection

You want to show the director that you can speak loudly and clearly onstage. The director will not cast you in a speaking role if he or she fears the audience will not be able to hear you. "Projection" is the term for speaking in such a way that your voice reaches the audience without your having to shout.

Characterization

Reciting a monologue is not like reading a textbook out loud in class. When performing a monologue, you are not just conveying information, you are also conveying a character. Make concrete choices about your character that will come across in your performance. For example, if your character is a star athlete, you will want to appear tough and confident. Stand up straight and take things in as if nothing can get you down.

Focal point

When delivering your monologue, try focusing on a point just above the audience members' heads. Looking someone directly in the eye could make that person uncomfortable, while looking off to the side or down at the floor could make you appear unsure of yourself.

Context

While some monologues are created on their own, most are originally sections of dialogue from an actual play or musical. To better understand your monologue, you may want to read the play from which it was taken. Get an idea of who your character is, who your character is talking to during the scene in which the monologue occurs, and what your character is trying to achieve during this scene. As you perform your monologue, keep an image of the character to which you are speaking in your mind's eye. Imagine that character's reactions as you speak to him or her, and your performance will appear more convincing.

You may be asked to read sides at the audition, rather than a prepared monologue. This means you will not have to select and

Although these actors have scripts in their hands, they are still reacting to one another. They appear engaged in the scene and thus are interesting to watch. Performances like this are sure to catch the director's attention during an audition.

memorize a monologue ahead of time. However, it is still a good idea to prepare for the audition by reading the script. This way, when you are handed a side to read, you will already be familiar with the scene from which it was taken. During these readings, you can expect the director to call your name and place you in a group of actors. Your group will then be assigned a particular side to read, with each member of the group reading a specific character's lines. If you are not asked to read for a part in which you are interested, it is best not to protest. If you do, the director could get the impression that you are difficult to work with. Instead, graciously accept the role you have been offered, and perform it to the best of your ability. If the director is impressed by your performance, he or she may ask you to read again, this time for a more sizable part.

Readings of sides are often referred to as "cold readings." This is because actors are not always given time to warm up, or rehearse their side, before taking the stage. At most, you will be allowed to review the side one or two times with your group before performing it for the director. If you are already familiar with the show, you will not have to spend these precious moments trying to figure out what is going on in the side. Instead, you can focus on "getting into character."

Getting into Character

The phrase "getting into character" refers to the process of channeling your character's persona and state of mind before performing.

Getting into character requires focusing all your thoughts and energy on the part you will be playing. Your personal cares will only interfere with this task, so make sure to leave them behind. By the time you take the stage, your character's hopes and fears should be the only thoughts in your head.

Singing and Dancing Auditions

For the singing portion of the audition, you will be asked to sing either a song from the show or a song of your own choosing. If the song is to be from the show, the vocal director will most likely teach you and the other actors the song during the audition. After learning the song as a group, each of you will be asked to sing the song on your own, while being accompanied by a pianist.

Singing a song of your choice means you will not only have to pick a song to perform, you will also have to bring sheet music for that song to the audition. While you are singing, the director and vocal director will take notes on the following:

Ability to carry a tune

"Carrying a tune" refers to a person's ability to sing a tune accurately. Most people have a fairly easy time carrying a tune. However, if

Songs help to tell a musical's story. Actors must therefore make sure they have their audience's full attention when they are singing. Notice how lively and in character these singers appear. No doubt their audience is interested in what they have to say!

you are concerned about this aspect of the audition, have a friend play a few notes on a piano while you sing along. Ask your friend to give you his or her honest feedback. Were you able to match your voice to the notes? The more practice you get before your audition, the easier it will be to carry a tune when it comes time for you to perform.

Projection

The audience will not want to have to strain to hear you sing. Even if you are self-conscious about your singing abilities, you must try to sing in a voice that can be heard from the back of the house, or theater seating. Of course, this does not mean you should shout. Your singing voice should be pleasant to the ear.

Enunciation

Good enunciation is the act of speaking clearly and concisely. Many people do not sing as clearly as they speak. In other words, they sing with poor enunciation. In musicals, the songs help to tell the story. Therefore, it is very important for the audience to understand the lyrics. Singing with good enunciation is probably more difficult than you think, so you should really concentrate on sounding out your words while performing your song.

Energy

Whether you are acting, singing, or dancing, it is important for you to have high energy. This means appearing positive, confident, and ready to perform! It also means no slouching, squirming, staring at your feet, or fidgeting, no matter how nervous you are. If you look like you have no confidence in yourself, your audience will assume you are not worth their attention.

Characterization

Just because you're singing doesn't mean you should stop playing a character. Work to become the character to which the song belongs. At the same time, ask yourself what the song is about and how the character should be feeling while singing it. If the song is about a lost love, singing with a big smile on your face will make your audience confused. If the song is happy, however, not smiling will seem just as strange.

Vocal range

Your vocal range is composed of all those notes you are able to sing comfortably. The more notes you can hit without straining, the larger your vocal range. Actors with small vocal ranges have trouble with songs that contain especially high or low notes. Therefore, actors who have large vocal ranges tend to be more desirable. Increasing your vocal range can be done, but it takes some solid practice. If you wish to accomplish this goal, you may want to work one-on-one with a vocal coach.

Vocal technique

The term "vocal technique" refers to the tools advanced singers use to make their voices sound especially rich. Examples of these tools include vibrato and belting. If you are not an accomplished singer, do not worry too much about exhibiting technique during the audition. It is more important that you sing clearly and in tune. Good vocal technique often takes quite some time to learn and must be taught by a proper voice teacher.

Even if the vocal director has asked you to bring your own song to the audition, he or she will still judge your performance based on the criteria above. Of course, in this case, you will have the opportunity to sing a song with which you are particularly comfortable. When choosing your own song, you can weed out numbers containing notes you can't quite hit, while at the same time considering pieces that show off your unique vocal abilities. In addition, if you choose your song at least several days before the audition, you will have some extra time to practice.

Choosing an audition song is a lot like choosing an audition monologue. If the show for which you are auditioning is an upbeat comedy, a lively, comedic song is a better choice than a dramatic ballad. If you are hoping to be cast in a role meant for a soprano, or a woman with a very high voice, you should make sure to pick a song that shows off your ability to hit high notes. Do some research in order to find out what show the song you choose is from and how the character to which it belongs behaves. If you sing as a

Prepare for the audition by singing along to a recording of your song. It is important that you know your song very well by the time of the audition.

specific character, you will be more interesting to watch than if you sing as your regular, everyday self.

The prospect of finding an audition song can seem difficult if you are unfamiliar with musical theater repertoire. Fortunately, there are books and Web sites designed to assist all actors, no matter what their level of experience, with this very task. On some Web sites, you can search for songs based on your age, the style of song you are looking for, and your vocal range.

Once you have settled on a song, you will want to purchase the sheet music. Sheet music is a printed copy of the notes and

Finding Your Vocal Range

In musical theater repertoire, vocal ranges are grouped into the following categories:

- Bass: A very low male voice
- Baritone: A low male voice
- Tenor: A medium-to-high male voice
- Alto: A low-to-medium female voice
- Mezzo: A medium-to-high female voice
- Soprano: A high female voice

If you are unsure which category you belong in, try listening to and singing along with a few songs written for various ranges. You can listen to songs online or by checking out CDs at your local library. The song you have the easiest time singing was likely written for your voice type.

lyrics to a song. The accompanist will read from your sheet music at the audition, so it is important that you bring it along. Otherwise, you will have to sing *a cappella*—on your own, without an accompanist. Come prepared, and you will be glad you did!

Once you learn your songs, you will need to practice singing them onstage. Singing on a stage is different from singing in a choir room. You will need to make sure that your voice, expression, and movements are big enough to be seen from the last row in the house.

Your Dance Audition

With singing out of the way, it is time for the dance audition. During the dance audition, the choreographer will teach you and the other actors a small dance segment from the show. After running through the dance several times all together, you and the other actors will be separated into small groups. Each group will be positioned into rows and will perform the dance once or twice for the choreographer and director. If you are an inexperienced dancer, hiding in the back row won't help you. The choreographer is going to see you no matter what, and if you look like you want to disappear, he or she is going to assume you don't

enjoy being onstage. This does not mean, however, that you should stand in the front row if you are feeling less than confident. If you feel there is a chance that you will forget the moves, stand behind a more experienced dancer so that you can follow him or her. No matter what, smile and hold your head high. If you have good energy onstage, you will at least look like you are willing to work hard and improve your dancing skills during the rehearsal process.

Whether you are acting onstage, sitting in the audience, waiting in the wings, or packing your things up and heading home, as long as you are at the audition, you are performing for the director. It is important to show him or her how mature, polite, and responsible you can be. If the director catches even the slightest glimpse of you whining, talking back, or not paying attention during the audition, he or she may decide that it's not worth it to cast you. No matter how talented you may be, you will never make it as an actor if you develop a reputation for being difficult.

By the time the audition is over, you should be proud of yourself. Try to view any mistakes you made as being learning experiences. They will only help you the second time around. For now, congratulate yourself on a job well done. Take some time to relax and look forward to the upcoming months—no matter what part in the show you receive, the rehearsal process is sure to be a lot of fun!

The Early Rehearsal Process

Now that the nerve-wracking audition process is complete, it's time to relax and have some fun at rehearsal. High school musicals typically rehearse for two months, so try to keep your after-school schedule as free as possible during this time.

You may have made it safely through tryouts, but it remains important for you to impress the director with your readiness, respect, and enthusiasm. Your part in the show is never completely safe. The director may choose to drop you at any time if he or she doesn't see you being a team player. Plus, your attitude is sure to be remembered the next time an audition rolls around. Keeping this in mind, here are some important tips regarding rehearsal etiquette:

Be on time

Arriving late for rehearsal tells the director you don't really want to be there. In addition, it wastes everyone's time—yours included!

Early in the rehearsal process, you and your fellow cast members will get together and run through the script. This is an excellent time to really begin to think about your character and how you will portray him or her.

Bring a pencil

At every rehearsal, you will have to take notes in your script. Therefore, be sure to bring a pencil with you. If you forget to bring one, don't expect the director to have extras. It's not his or her responsibility to provide you with a pencil.

Style yourself appropriately

It's a good idea to always come dressed as if you are auditioning. This means no high heels, no tight or baggy clothing, and keeping long hair out of your face. Inappropriate dressing could cause a painful accident, and how can you show off your fabulous acting skills from behind a curtain of hair?

Sit in the front of the house, or theater seating

From the back of the house, you won't be able to hear your director's instructions. Sitting in the back can also appear disrespectful. Professional, enthusiastic actors always sit toward the front of the house so that they can pay close attention to those in charge. Of course, you don't want to sit so close to the director and stage manager that you make them uncomfortable. Be sure to give them some space.

Never bring food and drink (other than water) into the theater

Unwrapping and chewing food can be loud and distracting to the people onstage.

If you need to leave the theater, let the director or stage manager know

If you're needed onstage and no one knows where you are, people will quickly become exasperated. Let the director or stage manager know if you need to use the restroom, and make sure to get back to the rehearsal as quickly as possible.

Never direct other actors

Remember, you are not the director. It can be tempting to give other cast members acting advice, especially if you don't agree with their choices. However, doing so is absolutely not your job. If someone truly needs coaching, you can trust that the director will take care of the situation.

Never second-guess the director

If you have a great idea related to your character, feel free to mention it to the director following the rehearsal. However, keep in mind that the director should always get the last word. Therefore, if he or she ultimately disagrees with you, it's best not to argue. It's the director's job to make final decisions about the show, not yours.

Quiet offstage!

Your fellow actors deserve to be heard. When you're not onstage, you should be sitting silently in the house, either watching the rehearsal or working on memorizing your lines.

Guard your script with your life and bring it to every rehearsal

Scripts cost money and can be difficult to come by. If you lose your script, you could cause your director quite a predicament. Your script is your single most important tool during the rehearsal process. Failure to treat it responsibly will hurt your stage reputation.

Although the entire cast will most likely come together for the first rehearsal, you probably won't be called for, or requested to attend, every rehearsal afterward. Being called depends on whether or not your character takes part in the scene being rehearsed. Usually, a director will hang a call sheet at a central location to announce the names of the actors called that week. Be sure to check the call sheet every day in case the director makes any changes to that week's rehearsal schedule.

The first rehearsal is a chance for you to meet the cast and crew, as well as to familiarize yourself with the show as a whole. Following introductions, you can expect to take part in a read-through, or a reading of the script during which each player reads his or her part out loud. It is important for even those actors without lines to follow along during the read-through. Every cast member must learn the musical's sequence of events, or "run of show."

There is no need to fret if you stumble over your lines during the read-through. Remember, this will be the cast's first time reading the entire script as a group. No one can be expected to be perfect already. However, do try your best to speak your lines with energy and conviction.

You will find that song lyrics are included in musical scripts. When you come to a song during a read-through, you will not be expected to sing. However, you might be expected to read the lyrics out loud if it's your character that is to be singing. In musicals, songs are important pieces of the story. Excluding them from the read-through will keep you and the rest of the cast from fully understanding the plot.

After orchestrating the initial read-through, the director will spend the next few weeks of rehearsal blocking the show. "Blocking" refers to movement onstage. During blocking rehearsals, the director will tell you when, where, and how to move. These are the types of rehearsals during which it is especially important to have a pencil. You must write your directions in the margins of your script so that the next time you rehearse the scene, you will know exactly where to go.

During blocking rehearsals, the director may use terms like "upstage" and "downstage" when telling you where to go. These terms are called stage directions and refer to the various parts of a stage. See the diagram on page 33 for help with understanding these directions. The diagram is drawn from the audience's point of view.

"Stage right" is on the audience's left, and "stage left" is on the audience's right. This is because these directions are defined according to the actor's point of view. If the director tells you to "cross downstage right," you will know to move to your right, as well as toward the audience.

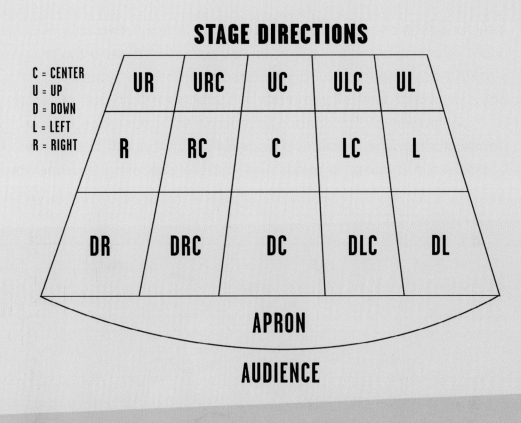

STAGE DIRECTIONS

C = CENTER
U = UP
D = DOWN
L = LEFT
R = RIGHT

UR	URC	UC	ULC	UL
R	RC	C	LC	L
DR	DRC	DC	DLC	DL

APRON

AUDIENCE

This diagram represents the various areas of the stage. You can use the abbreviations listed here when writing down your blocking. For example, if the director asks you to cross downstage right, you can write "X DR" in your script, rather than writing out a long sentence.

As the director gives you your blocking, make sure you understand the motivation behind every move you make. If you do not know why your character is moving a certain way, you will appear awkward onstage and your confusion will be made known to the audience. Let the director know if you are confused about your motivation. He or she should be able to clear things up for you.

While some actors are attending blocking rehearsals, others will be learning song and dance numbers with either the vocal director or the choreographer. Most likely, these rehearsals will occur in areas outside the theater, so as not to disturb those working on blocking. Vocal rehearsals often take place in a band or choir room, where there is a piano for the vocal director or accompanist to play. Dance rehearsals will take place in a dance studio, where you and your fellow actors can watch yourselves in a mirror to make sure you are executing your moves

One of the most challenging parts of a musical performance is staying in character while you sing.

appropriately. It is important to pay as much attention and respect to the vocal director and choreographer as you would to the director. If they are displeased with your behavior, they will make it known to the director and your part in the show could become at risk.

Staying in Character

If you think singing and dancing have nothing to do with acting, you're wrong. You must stay in character, even when hitting a high note or performing a pirouette. A dramatic ballad must be filled with a character's emotion in order for the audience to connect with it. A comedic dance number should be just as hilarious as a comedic monologue.

These actors are playing specific characters while executing choreographed dance moves. Take a look at their facial expressions. Do you think they are doing a good job staying in character?

Learn your musical numbers so well that you could sing and dance your way through the show in your sleep. Once songs and choreography are transferred to the stage, you will no longer have a mirror to focus on or a piano positioned close to your ear. At this point, it will become especially important for you to exercise your concentration skills.

After a long day of rehearsal, you may be tempted to go home and relax—and it's important to do so! However, rehearsing a high school musical does not begin and end at school. There is some homework for you to do as well.

Developing Your Character and Learning Your Lines

One thing the director cannot teach you is how to truly become your character. This you must do on your own, and it is not something you can expect to occur magically onstage. Becoming acquainted with your character is something that requires a good deal of personal time and effort, usually outside of rehearsal.

As soon as you receive your script, you should start taking some time each day to look it over while thinking seriously about your character. For the next two to three months, you will be required to be this person for up to several hours a day. It is important that you get to know him or her. Of course, there's only so much you can learn about your character from reading a script. Knowledge of certain details will have to come from somewhere else: your imagination. That's right—it's up to you to pick up where the playwright left off and finish piecing together your character. This process is necessary to the craft of acting, and it is called character development.

The more you know about your character, the more developed your character will become. A developed character is much more interesting to the audience and gives the other actors onstage more to work with. Most important, a developed character is someone with whom you will be able to build a strong connection. Once this takes place, you will see your character start to come to life.

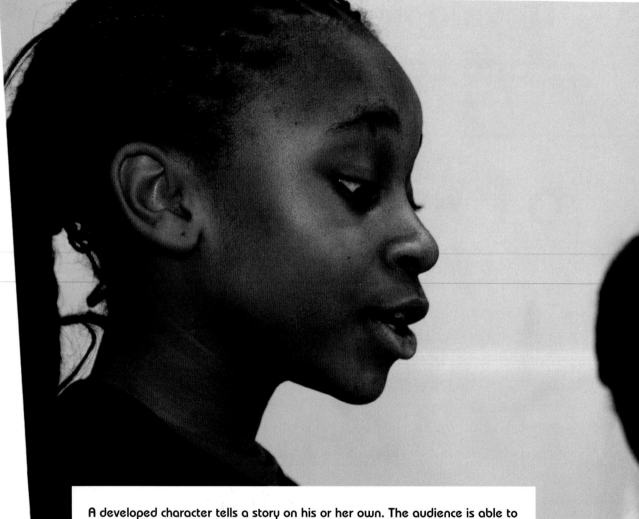

A developed character tells a story on his or her own. The audience is able to connect with the character's likes and dislikes, hopes for the future, and deepest concerns. You want your character to be just as real to your audience.

So, how exactly does character development work? There are many different methods to executing this creative task. Let's examine a few, using the character of the wicked stepmother from *Snow White* as an example.

Right away, you know two things about the wicked stepmother. One: she's wicked. Two: she's a stepmother. After reading the script, you obviously learn a little bit more. For instance, you learn that she's jealous of her stepdaughter's beauty. You learn that she disguises herself as a poor old woman and gives her stepdaughter a poisoned apple. But surely there's more to her than these simple facts. It's time this stepmother was developed!

Try conducting an interview with the wicked stepmother in order to get to know her on an intimate level. You can play both roles during this interview: that of the interviewer and that of the interviewee. The questions you ask can be seemingly random, such as, "What do you usually have for breakfast?" Questions like these may seem pointless, but they can actually tell you a lot about a person. For instance, you may decide that the wicked stepmother has one dozen doughnuts for breakfast every day. In your mind,

Pick a quiet place to interview your character. Write down a series of questions, or simply ask your character whatever comes to your mind. Make sure you write down your character's answers. You will want to refer back to them so you remember what kind of person you have developed.

she is a truly depressed stepmother and is using food to try and fill a void in her life. Or, you may decide that the wicked stepmother doesn't eat breakfast at all. She simply doesn't have time to eat, as she's far too focused on hatching yet another evil plan. By simply considering the wicked stepmother's choice in breakfast foods, you have already created for her two possible personalities: she is

either a sad, pitiful person that feels there is something missing in her life, or she is a frenzied, determined person who is unable to focus on more than one thing at a time.

While conducting your interview, you can also ask your character questions you have been sincerely wondering yourself, such as, "Do you ever feel guilty about being so wicked?" Putting yourself in the stepmother's shoes, you may decide that her answer is, "Not at all! I don't consider myself to be 'wicked' in the first place! It's that brat Snow White that's wicked! She may act sweet and innocent, but really she's a devious person who is competing with me for my husband's attention. She simply must be stopped!" How's that for a wealth of background information?

Questions about a character's past are also excellent interview options. The famous actor and director Constantin Stanislavsky once said, "There can be no present without a past." In other words, it is the past that makes a character the person he or she is today. If an actor wants to understand who his character is, he must first understand who his character was.

Stanislavsky also said, about the future, "An actor should always have before him thoughts about the future."

What do you think about when you ponder the future? Maybe you daydream about your goals and aspirations. For your character, it's the same. When the wicked stepmother thinks about the future, it is possible that she is imaging how pleasant things will be once Snow White is no longer the fairest in the land.

Everything you or your character says and does is based on a desire for the future, or an objective. Objectives can be defined using "I want" statements, such as, "I want to be healthier" or "I want to get an 'A' in biology."

Objectives are then fulfilled using tactics. Tactics for the above objectives might be to lift weights or to take notes.

Discovering your character's objectives will help you to connect with his or her desires. In addition, it will make your acting more believable. If you perform a tactic with a certain objective in mind, you will be more convincing to the audience.

Character development is not the only task you must take on outside of rehearsal. Right away, you must work on memorizing your lines. The most common technique for line memorization is

Questions for Your Character

If you are having trouble coming up with interview questions, here are nineteen to get you started. They can be asked of any character. Written by Entertainment Software Association vice president Rich Taylor, these questions were originally developed for role-playing gamers. However, they work just as well for role-playing actors!

- What is your birth name? What name do you use?
- What are your parents like?
- What is your first memory?
- Who is your best friend?
- What is your fondest childhood memory? Your worst?
- What were you like in high school?
- Who was your idol when you were growing up?
- What hobbies do you have?
- Who is your worst enemy? Why don't you get along?
- What would be the perfect gift for you?
- What type of weather is your favorite? Why?
- What is your favorite animal? Why?
- What kinds of things embarrass you? Why?
- What one act in your past are you most ashamed of? Proud of?
- When was the last time you cried?
- What's the worst injury you ever received? How did it happen?
- What is your current short-term goal?
- What is your current long-term goal?
- How private of a person are you? Why?

called running lines. Running lines consists of speaking your lines out loud while being prompted by a partner. Anyone, even your mom or dad, can help you to run your lines. Hand your script to the person of your choice, and ask him or her to read your cues out loud. Cues are the lines that take place right before you speak. They should serve as signals that it is time for you to say a certain

Find time outside of rehearsal to run lines with other cast members. You can take turns reciting lines and giving cues. It is best to devote at least half an hour a day to running your lines.

line. If you have highlighted your lines in your script, it should be easy for your partner to locate your cues. They will be the lines right above each highlighted section. If you can't remember a line, you can say, "Line," to your partner. Your partner will then read the beginning of your next line to you, as a hint. Run your lines until you can make it through the entire scene without any errors several times in a row.

Actors sometimes test how well they have memorized their lines by conducting a "speed-through." A speed-through is similar to a read-through. In this exercise, you and the other actors will recite the musical's lines and song lyrics together, with each actor speaking the words belonging to his or her part. However, during a speed-through, there are no scripts allowed. Together, you and your fellow cast members will work to make your way through the play from memory as quickly as possible. During a speed-through, you will not be expected to be in character, as you should be entirely focused on recalling your lines. Reciting lines from memory is difficult as it is. If you manage to do so at top speed, you can consider yourself ready to stop relying on your script!

Both character development and line memorization are ongoing tasks. You will continue to work on them throughout the beginning stages of the rehearsal process. However, there will soon come a time to set your script aside and put your character development to the test. Your hard work will truly take the stage during the run-through and dress rehearsals.

On With the Show!

Once scenes have been blocked, songs have been learned, and choreography has been put into place, you will begin to attend run-through rehearsals. During these rehearsals, a string of scenes is acted out onstage, complete with blocking, singing, and dancing. Scripts will be allowed for the first few run-through rehearsals, but soon the cast will be "off book," meaning scripts will no longer be allowed onstage.

Run-Through Rehearsals

Run-through rehearsals can be a lot of fun. Since you aren't stopping to record blocking, the rehearsals will move more quickly. You will have more time to develop your character, and your part will start to come to life. Without a script, you will have more freedom of movement. You will be able to make constant eye contact with your fellow actors and will be better able to connect with them. However, you may find that without a script to hold, you're suddenly unsure of what to do with your hands. This common problem among actors often leads to fidgeting. Unless your character is supposed to be nervous, fidgeting never looks good onstage. The best thing to do in this type of situation is to relax. Try not to think about how awkward you feel. Instead, concentrate on the

Because they don't have scripts in their hands, these actors are able to use body language to help tell a story and bring their characters to life. Based on the body language you see here, what do you think is going on in this scene?

scene at hand and simply do what comes naturally. Do something with your hands that your character might do in order to avoid fidgeting.

Once you are officially off book, you will attend a few rehearsals at which you will be allowed to call for a line. During these rehearsals, if you forget a line, you may call, "Line!" to the stage manager, who

will most likely be sitting in the house. The stage manager will then read the beginning of your line to you, as a reminder. Calling for a line should be treated as a last resort. Before you do so, give yourself a few moments to see if you can recall the line on your own. Relying only on the stage manager will make you unprepared for the time when he or she can no longer come to your rescue.

It is likely that you will forget a line when you can no longer call for one. If this happens, do not panic. No one is going to be angry if you handle the situation properly. Professional actors forget their lines all the time. One sign of a skilled actor is how well he or she can recover from dropping a line. The key is never to let the audience know. Rather than becoming visibly upset and breaking character, keep playing your part as if nothing unfortunate has happened. You may ad-lib, or make up lines on the spur of the moment, to replace the lines you have forgotten. As long as you keep the story moving forward, the audience will never know the difference. If you are having trouble ad-libbing, another option is to skip to the next line you do know, provided that this doesn't mean skipping over a significant portion of the scene. Skipping a page or more of dialogue is never a good idea. The audience will become confused, as will the other actors.

If another actor has forgotten his or her lines, you can use your ad-libbing skills to keep the scene moving. You can even say the actor's line for him or her by prefacing it with, "I know what you're thinking," or, "Weren't you just saying the other day . . ." Again, if this is done effectively, the audience won't know a mistake was made.

Dress Rehearsals

Once the cast is able to run through the show smoothly, it's time for lights, sound, and costumes! In other words, it's time for the dress rehearsal. Stage actors always look forward to the dress rehearsal process. During this rehearsal, or series of rehearsals, actors run through the show in complete hair, makeup, and costumes. In addition, the crew works to execute full lighting, sound, and set changes. The only thing missing from the show during a dress rehearsal is the audience.

Dress rehearsals always give a musical an exciting new feel. Costumes, lighting, and sets make scenes feel like real life! Let these exciting new elements help you get into character.

You will find that once you put on your costume, you will feel much more in character. As the entire cast experiences this phenomenon, dress rehearsals often receive an extra boost of positive energy. However, costumes and props can also be distracting at first, resulting in dropped lines, late entrances, and other minor setbacks. Just keep in mind that these mistakes are necessary for learning to ad-lib, change costumes, and work with props and sets with confidence.

Dress rehearsals can run one or even two hours longer than other rehearsals. This is partly because you and your fellow actors will need extra time to put on your costumes and makeup. These preparations usually take place backstage, in a designated dressing room. Most often, there are only two dressing rooms: one for boys, and one for girls. With all the hustle and bustle that takes place before a show, dressing rooms can become pretty chaotic. Try to arrive at the dressing room as early as possible so that you can put yourself together before the other actors take over. Once the crowd settles in, mirror, shelf, and changing space will become scarce.

When changing in the dressing room, always hang your costumes. If you feel you don't have time to hang a costume before you're due back onstage, have a friend hang it for you. Costumes left on the floor may become ruined or misplaced. At the very least, they will become terribly wrinkled. It is also important not to eat or drink in costume, as you could spill something and stain what you're wearing.

You may be required to perform a quick change, which is a change of costume that must take place in about five minutes or less. Some quick changes must be done in less than thirty seconds! These changes leave no time for rushing back to the dressing room, so you will have to change in the wings. Ask if the crew can set up an enclosed area where you can dress in privacy. Enlist a fellow actor to help you with any zippers and buttons.

The dress rehearsal will also be the first time you rehearse with a full technical crew backstage. Working under the direction of the stage manager, the tech crew handles behind-the-scenes tasks like pulling the curtain, placing the props, and changing the set. It is important for you to treat the tech crew with respect, as they are working just as hard as you are to make sure the show is a success. Be sure to stay out of their way as they move heavy objects on and off the stage. The tech crew is instructed to make sure everything runs smoothly backstage.

Following run-through and dress rehearsals, the director will call you and the other actors into the house. He or she will then give notes on the performance. You may be told you are doing an incredible job! You also may be told that you need to speak up, that your character needs work, or that your blocking is all wrong. Do not take criticism too personally. The director has faith in you and is simply trying to help you do your best. Take notes on what he or she says, and during the next rehearsal, work to put the advice you were given into practice.

Sooner or later, the very last dress rehearsal will come to an end, meaning it's time to perform for a live audience. At this point, you can expect to be a little nervous, but you should not let your nerves frighten you. This feeling is perfectly natural and is not a sign that you are unprepared or that something bad is going to happen. In fact, nervousness can be a good thing! It increases your adrenaline, giving you an extra boost of energy. Use this energy to really give your performance your all. Also, remember that the audience members are not there to laugh at or criticize you. They are there to be entertained.

During the show, it is entirely up to you to make each of your entrances and exits on time. If you are quiet backstage, you should be able to hear what is happening onstage. Once you hear lines

Places!

When you are in the dressing room preparing for a show, expect tech crew members to stop by and let you know how much time there is before the curtain goes up. "Fifteen minutes until the house is open!" a crew member will call. And you will know that in fifteen minutes, audience members will be allowed to take their seats. Someone shouting,

Before making an entrance, you will wait in the wings, or the sides of the stage just outside the audience's view. Usually, the tech crew will mark sight lines, or the points at which actors are not visible, on the floor of the wings using white tape. When in the wings, make sure to stand behind the marked sight line.

"Five minutes until the house is open!" tells you that in five minutes, you had better be quiet or the audience will hear you warming up your voice and chatting with your friends. When you finally hear, "The house is open!" no more talking is allowed. On the other side of the curtain, the audience is filing in, anticipating your big debut. Soon, minutes will be called again. "Ten minutes until places!" a crew member will shout, informing you that if you're in the first scene, you must either be in the wings or onstage in just ten minutes. Make sure your hair is in place, your costume is on straight, and that your nerves are under control. Finally, "Places!" will be called, and you can consider it showtime! Hurry to your position and wait just a few seconds for the curtain to come up and the lights to come on.

or songs from the scene before your next entrance, silently take your place in the wings and await your cue.

Prior to making an entrance, you may find it helpful to relax and get into character in a quiet corner backstage. Find a spot where you can be by yourself and close your eyes. Release the tension in your body, one muscle at a time. Run through your lines in your head, and focus on your character. What was he or she doing right before the scene you are about to perform? How is he or she feeling now? Leave your own thoughts behind, including your nervousness about taking the stage.

When the curtain goes down on your very first show, no doubt you will hardly be able to wait for it to go up again. Very little is more exhilarating than being an actor in a live musical. As you continue to audition, rehearse, and perform, you will continue to mature, learn, and grow as an actor. Show business certainly isn't easy, but the payoff is absolutely worth it. No doubt you will soon find out that like they say, "There's no business like show business!"

GLOSSARY

a cappella Without instrumental accompaniment.

accompanist A musician, usually a pianist, who plays along with a vocalist.

adrenaline A hormone that is produced during stressful or exhilarating situations. It raises the heart rate and dilates blood vessels.

audition A performance given before a small group of people who determine if and where a person should be placed in the cast of a play.

autograph A celebrity's signature, often considered a collectible.

ballad A slow, dramatic song.

blocking A chart for the placement and movement of stage performers.

characterization How an actor represents a character.

choreographer The person who determines the movements of the dancers in a musical performance.

dialogue The written conversation between two characters.

enunciation To say or sing each syllable of a word carefully, in order to be understood.

lead A character that plays a major part in telling the play or musical's story.

lines Segments of theatrical dialogue belonging to a specific character.

lyrics The words to a song.

monologue Lengthy dialogue spoken by only one character.

persona A person's visible attitude or demeanor.

pirouette A ballet move consisting of a 360-degree turn on one leg.

playwright The writer of a play.

projection Control over a voice that ensures good volume, clarity, and enunciation.

props Objects used to help tell a story or convey a character.

repertoire A list or supply of artistic works.

script A book containing the lines and lyrics to a show.

thespian A person that is enthusiastic about theater.

triple threat A performer who is an accomplished singer, dancer, and actor.

wings The sides of the stage from which actors enter.

Academy of Motion Picture Arts and Sciences Academy Foundation

8949 Wilshire Boulevard
Beverly Hills, CA 90211
(310) 247-3000
Web site: http://www.oscars.org
This organization hosts the Academy Awards, or Oscars.

Actors' Equity National Headquarters

165 West 46th Street
New York, NY 10036
(212) 869-8530
Web site: http://www.actorsequity.org
This labor union represents American actors and stage managers in the theater.

American Alliance for Theatre and Education

4811-B Saint Elmo Avenue
Bethesda, MD 20814
(301) 951-7977
Web site: http://www.aate.com
This organization supports theater educators, such as high school drama teachers.

Broadway League

226 West 47th Street
New York, NY 10036

(212) 764-1122
Web site: http://www.broadwayleague.com
This is an association of Broadway theater owners, operators, producers, and performers.

A Minor Consideration

14530 Denker Avenue
Gardena, CA 90247
Web site: http://www.minorcon.org
This organization is dedicated to supporting young performers.

Screen Actors Guild

5757 Wilshire Boulevard, 7th Floor
Los Angeles, CA 90036-3600
(323) 954-1600
Web site: http://www.sag.org
This labor union represents American television and film actors.

Web Sites

Due to the changing nature of Internet links, Rosen Publishing has developed an online list of Web sites related to the subject of this book. This site is updated regularly. Please use this link to access the list:

http://www.rosenlinks.com/hsm/act

FOR FURTHER READING

Belli, Mary Lou, and Dinah Lenney. *Acting for Young Actors: The Ultimate Teen Guide*. New York, NY: Back Stage Books, 2006.

Brady Johnson, Maureen. *Middle Mania: Imaginative Theater Projects for Middle School Actors*. Lynne, NH: Smith and Kraus, 2001.

Lamedman, Debbie. *A Teen Actor's Guide to Laying the Foundation for a Successful Acting Career*. Lynne, NH: Smith and Kraus, 2007.

Silverberg, Larry. *The 7 Simple Truths of Acting for the Teen Actor*. Lynne, NH: Smith and Kraus, 2007.

Stevens, Chambers. *Magnificent Monologues for Teens: The Teens' Monologue Source for Every Occasion*. Pasadena, CA: Sandcastle Publishing, 2002.

Bruder, Melissa, Lee Michael Cohn, Madeline Olnek, Nathaniel Pollack, Robert Previto, and Scott Zigler. *A Practical Handbook for the Actor*. New York, NY: A Vintage Original, 1986.

Meisner, Sanford, and Dennis Longwell. *On Acting*. New York, NY: A Vintage Original, 1987.

MusicalTheatreAudition.com. Retrieved August 13, 2008 (http://www.musicaltheatreaudition.com/joomla).

Musical-Theatre-Kids.com. "Stage Directions for Actors." Retrieved August 13, 2008 (http://www.musical-theater-kids.com/images/stage-directions-1.jpg).

Oliver, Donald. *How to Audition for the Musical Theatre*. Lynne, NH: Smith and Kraus, 1995.

Schreiber, Terry. *Acting: Advanced Techniques for the Actor, Director, and Teacher*. New York, NY: Allworth Press, 2005.

Stanislavsky, Constantin. *Creating a Role*. New York, NY: Routledge, 1961.

Taylor, Rich. "The Original 100 Questions Essay Test for Character Development." Retrieved September 3, 2008 (http://skitten.best.vwh.net/100questions.html).

INDEX

About the Author

As a high school senior, Bethany Bezdecheck and her twin sister had the opportunity to direct their own play, which went on to become an award-winning entry at California's Lanaea Theatre Festival. Today, Bezdecheck writes on a number of nonfiction topics and lives in New Jersey with her husband and her dog.

Photo Credits

Cover (background), p. 1 Torsten Blackwood/AFP/Getty Images; cover (inset), p. 34 Emmanuel Faure/Stone/Getty Images; pp. 4–5 Gareth Cattermole/Getty Images; pp. 8–9 © Caroline Chen/Syracuse Newspapers/The Image Works; p. 11 © Sjkold/The Image Works; p. 13 © Syracuse Newspapers/G. Wright/The Image Works; pp. 18–19 © Jim West/Photo Edit; p. 22 © Bonnie Kamin/Photo Edit; pp. 24–25 © Cindy Charles/Photo Edit; pp. 28–29 © Spencer Grant/Photo Edit; pp. 35, 51 © Peter Hvizdak/The Image Works; pp. 38–39 © Jim West/ The Image Works; pp. 40–41 Shutterstock.com; pp. 44–45 © Bill Aron/ Photo Edit; pp. 48–49 © Will Hart/Photo Edit; p. 54 © Sean Clayton/ The Image Works.

Designer: Sam Zavieh; Editor: Bethany Bryan
Photo Researcher: Cindy Reiman